20TH CENTURY · DESIGN

20s AND 30s

BETWEEN THE WARS

was produced by

David West ✶✶ Children's Books
7 Princeton Court
55 Felsham Road
London SW15 1AZ

Picture Research: Brooks Krikler Research

First published in Great Britain in 1999 by
Heinemann Library, Halley Court, Jordan Hill,
Oxford OX2 8EJ, a division of Reed Educational and
Professional Publishing Limited.

OXFORD MELBOURNE AUCKLAND
JOHANNESBURG BLANTYRE GABORONE
IBADAN PORTSMOUTH (NH) USA CHICAGO

03 02 01
10 9 8 7 6 5 4 3 2

ISBN 0 431 03952 6 (HB)
ISBN 0 431 03953 4 (PB)

British Library Cataloguing in Publication Data

Gaff, Jackie
Between wars (1920s - 1930s). - (Design in the
twentieth century)
1. Design - History - 20th century - Juvenile literature
I. Title
745.4'442

Printed and bound in Italy

*The dates in brackets after a designer's
name give the years that he or she lived.
Where a date appears after an object (or, in
the case of a building, the town where it is
situated), it is the year of its design.
'C.' stands for circa, meaning about or
approximately.*

*An explanation of difficult words can be
found in the glossary on page 30*

20TH CENTURY · DESIGN

20s AND 30s

BETWEEN THE WARS

Jackie Gaff

Heinemann
LIBRARY

CONTENTS

Art deco was the supreme decorative arts style of the '20s and '30s – seen here in the stylized shapes and geometric patterns of a sculpture from the famous Parisian music hall, the Folies-Bergère.

Unemployment rocketed in the '30s, and the breadlines formed by people queuing up for food handouts were a common sight in cities the world over.

CHANGING TIMES

The 1920s and '30s were decades of constant change and development, as people emerged from the horrors of World War I and struggled to forge a new era of peace and progress. The desire for a fresh start encouraged new ideas, and architects and designers were inspired by the challenge of using new materials to shape a modern way of life.

Streamline styling was applied to all forms of transport including steam trains like this Hudson J-3a ('38).

In political and economic terms the two decades were also a time of change – but not always for the better. The early '20s saw many nations struggling to deal with large war debts and rising inflation. Then, in October '29, came the collapse of the New York stock exchange in the Wall Street Crash. The resulting economic depression caused appalling hardship, first in the United States and then throughout Europe.

On the political front, in many countries it was a period of repression and authoritarian rule by dictators, as fascism took hold under Benito Mussolini in Italy, Adolf Hitler in Germany, and Francisco Franco in Spain. The decades that had opened with such optimism closed in the devastating turmoil of another world war.

Many women worked for the first time during the war, and this gave rise to new financial and social independence. Hemlines rose and clothes became simpler and more practical, as women expressed their new-found sense of freedom.

The experimental climax of the post-war years were the futuristic designs shown at the New York World's Fair of '39.

FASHION

The war years had brought new social and financial freedom to women, and the 1920s was a time to celebrate this with the invention of a totally new look. Women were leading more active lives, and they wanted clothes and hairstyles to match. The fussiness of the pre-war years dropped away, as women cropped their hair into easy-to-manage, boyish bobs and began wearing the kind of shorter, loose-fitting garments that allowed far greater freedom of movement.

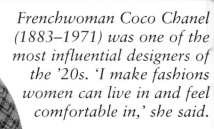

Athletic new dance crazes such as the Charleston, shown in this contemporary illustration, expressed the energy and freedom of the '20s.

Frenchwoman Coco Chanel (1883–1971) was one of the most influential designers of the '20s. 'I make fashions women can live in and feel comfortable in,' she said.

Chanel's easy-to-wear look included drop-waisted dresses, and cardigan jackets worn with pleated skirts.

Men also adopted more relaxed styles. Suits were cut more loosely, and made in softer fabrics.

FASHION HITS THE HIGH STREET

The new look was accompanied by wider availability. A range of new women's magazines and journals made it easier to pick up on the latest trends, while designer styles were made far more affordable through sewing and knitting patterns, and low-cost, department store copies.

The design revolution of the post-war years went hand in glove with technological developments. Often the material itself wasn't new – what was innovative was the technology that put it into mass-production.

Discovered in 1892 and named in 1924, rayon was the first artificial fabric. It was in great demand from the '20s onwards as a low-cost alternative to silk.

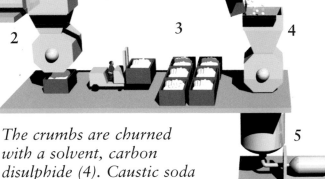

The viscose is aged and filtered (6), then vacuum-treated to remove air bubbles (7). Next it is forced through spinnerets into a spin bath of sulphuric acid (8), and lastly, the finished rayon yarn is spooled (9).

Cellulose sheets are soaked in caustic soda (1), then broken into crumbs (2) and aged for up to three days (3).

The crumbs are churned with a solvent, carbon disulphide (4). Caustic soda then dissolves the mixture to make viscose (5).

Close-up of spinneret

Tennis star Suzanne Lenglen epitomized the liberated look and lifestyle of the period.

MATERIAL GAINS

Fashion for all was made even more feasible by mass-production of rayon, the first artificial fabric. Rayon reproduced something of the luxury of silk at a fraction of the price, and it was made into a whole range of garments, from underwear to evening dresses.

WOMANLY WAYS

By the late '20s, the shapeless, boyish look was being replaced by styles that emphasized a sleek, feminine body shape. Hemlines dropped, and clothes were cut to cling to every curve. Streamlined fashions did not leave room for bulges, and a lightweight girdle made from the newly developed, elastic fibre Lastex was essential!

FANTASY FASHION

The most innovative fashion designer of the '30s was Italian-born Elsa Schiaparelli (1890–1973). Some of her strangest creations were made with her friend the surrealist Salvador Dalí (1904–89), and included a hat shaped like a shoe, a dress with a life-sized red lobster design, and lip-shaped pocket trims for a suit jacket.

Schiaparelli's surreal hen hat ('38) – its brim is the bird's nest!

ARCHITECTURE – MODERNISM

Above all else, the radical architects of the post-war years strove for simplicity. Buildings were reduced to basic geometric shapes, and where possible construction work was made easier by the use of prefabricated components. These were new buildings for a new age, and the style became known as modernism.

With its white concrete walls and metal-framed windows, this 1927 house is a classic modernist design.

SCHOOL OF THOUGHT

The German design school the Bauhaus was at the heart of modernism. It was founded in 1919 by the German-born architect Walter Gropius (1883–1969) to train artists to design for industrial production, but it became as famous for its theories as for its students. One of the key Bauhaus ideas was that form should follow function – that the appearance of an object or building should be determined by its use or purpose.

LE CORBUSIER

One of the most radical architects of the period, the Frenchman Le Corbusier (1887–1965) was fascinated by the machine, and once declared that 'the house is a machine for living in'. He took full advantage of reinforced concrete in constructing the framework of his buildings – this removed the need for walls to bear the weight of floors and roofs, and allowed for huge windows and open-plan interiors.

This model is of Le Corbusier's famous building the Villa Savoye (Paris, 1929–31), which was partly inspired by the deck of an ocean liner.

The new Bauhaus School Building (Dessau, Germany, '26) was designed by its director, Walter Gropius.

8

SIMPLE TASTES

One way of interpreting this theory was to keep decoration to a minimum, and the work of leading modernist architects such as Le Corbusier, Walter Gropius and German-born Mies van der Rohe (1886–1969) was certainly frill free. Buildings had flat roofs, window frames were prefabricated in metal (a cheaper alternative to labour-intensive wood), and walls were usually made from concrete. The form was stark, too, and dominated by geometric shapes such as cubes and rectangles.

MACHINES FOR LIVING

Buildings had become as streamlined and functional as that post-war symbol of speed and progress, the machine. The machine even stood for democracy, since mass-production meant that because products could be made more cheaply, they were available to more people.

Architects believed that everyone had the right to a well-designed house. The workers' homes at Weissenhofsiedlung (Stuttgart, Germany, '27) were designed by leading modernist architects, including Walter Gropius and Le Corbusier.

BUCKMINSTER FULLER

An engineer by training, Richard Buckminster Fuller (1895–1983) was a madly inventive American designer whose creative interests ranged from houses to cars. His architectural work bore no resemblance to the spare lines of modernists such as Le Corbusier. However, he was equally fascinated by the machine and mass-production, and applied the structural design of cars and aircraft to houses. His Dymaxion House ('27) was constructed from prefabricated units.

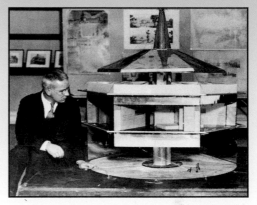

Buckminster Fuller poses beside his futuristic Dymaxion House.

9

SKYSCRAPERS

Architects were not only inspired by the idea of building new houses – they wanted to reinvent entire cities. And the city of the future needed a special kind of building, the skyscraper.

PAVING THE WAY

Two 19th-century technological developments had made skyscraper construction possible. One innovation was designing for a metal skeleton that could support walls as well as floors – this was first used in a Chicago skyscraper in 1883. The other was the invention of the electric lift in 1889.

10

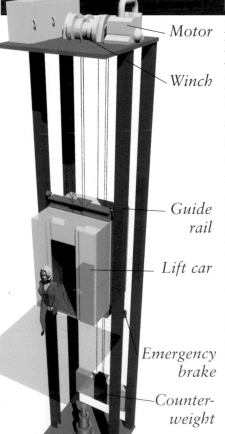

Motor

Winch

Guide rail

Lift car

Emergency brake

Counter-weight

LIFT-OFF!

Modern lifts are either hydraulic (driven by the pressure of a liquid) or electric, but because hydraulic lifts are slower they are not often used in tall skyscrapers. Today, the fastest electric lifts speed upwards at more than 600 metres per minute. In an electric lift, the car runs up and down on guide rails, or in a guide tower. The electric motor does not have to pull the whole load, because a counterweight rises as the car falls, and then helps to pull it back up again.

Completed in 1931, New York's 381-metre-high Empire State Building remained the world's tallest building for 40 years.

Working without safety lines or helmets, building workers risked their lives daily. As today, the steel sections of a skyscraper's framework were bolted and welded together like the pieces of a giant Meccano set.

In Lang's futuristic Metropolis, *road bridges connect a forest of gleaming skyscrapers.*

FUTURE WORLD

The German director Fritz Lang's 1926 film *Metropolis* creates a nightmarish future, in which a large section of the population live as slaves. The film's moral message is that technology may pose a threat to humanity, and its amazing futuristic sets were inspired by a visit Lang made to New York.

REACHING FOR THE SKIES

Although neither the technology nor the skyscraper was new, they truly came into their own in the 1920s and '30s. Until the Wall Street Crash put a spanner in the building boom, architects were inspired to design ever-more daring buildings that soared higher and higher into the skies.

JEWELS IN THE CROWN

Two of the most stunning post-war skyscrapers were built in New York. The Chrysler Building was designed by William Van Alen (1883–1954) and completed in 1930. Although it was never used by the company, it was commissioned by Chrysler motorcars and the fabulous art deco decoration towards the top was inspired by the latest car designs. At 320 metres high, it was for a short time the world's tallest building. In '31 it lost the title to the 381-metre-high Empire State Building, designed by Richmond H. Shreve (1877–1946), William Lamb (1883–1952) and Arthur Loomis Harmon (1878–1958).

The top of the Chrysler Building (New York, 1928–30) was clad in steel, one of the most popular materials of the period.

ART DECO STYLE

Art deco was the decorative face of 1920s and '30s style. In contrast to the sinuously curling plant and animal motifs of art nouveau, art deco was abstract and sharp edged. Colours were vibrantly hot and bright, and geometric shapes and patterns dominated, while inspiration was drawn from civilizations then considered exotic – Ancient Eygpt, the Aztecs, the Mayans and tribal Africa.

The expensive wood veneer and metal inlay, and the Egyptian lotus-flower motif of these lift doors from New York's Chrysler Building are the height of art deco luxury (William Van Alen, 1928–30).

The discovery of Tutankhamun's tomb in '22 prompted a craze for all things Egyptian.

ART DECO-RATION

Favourite art deco motifs were the chevron (a v-shape), pyramid, fan, lightning flash and sunray, as well as stylized waves, flowers and palm trees and speeding cars, planes and trains. They were used to decorate public buildings such as cinemas, restaurants and launderettes inside and out, but they also filtered down to '30s suburban homes, where the sunray motif was particularly popular for metal gates and in stained-glass insets to windows and doors.

Launched in 1932, the French liner Normandie *glittered with art deco style. These lacquered panels were created by the designer and craftsman, Jean Dunand (1877–1942).*

The exterior and interior of the Chanin Building (New York, '29) were decorated with art deco motifs. This executive suite bathroom is awash with geometric patterns and metal-and-glass detailing.

FOCUS POINT

Art deco takes its name from an international exhibition of decorative arts held in Paris in '25, the *Exposition Internationale des Arts Décoratifs et Industriels Modernes.* The style had been growing gradually and did not begin at exactly this time. However, the exhibition was attended by people from all over the world and it played a huge role in defining art deco and spreading its influence.

The geometric shape of the Hoover Factory was modernist, but its severity was softened by Egyptian-style art deco motifs (Wallis, Gilbert & Partners, London, '33).

LIGHT FANTASTIC

Modernist rooms were spacious, clutterfree and filled with light – it streamed in through huge windows, poured out from electric fittings, and bounced off white walls, mirrors, and chrome or stainless steel furnishings.

TURNING ON THE POWER

Electric light was still a symbol of modernity in the post-war years. The first power stations had begun operating in London and New York in 1882, but it was some time before national grid systems were established and low-cost electricity was made available to most people's homes.

Bauhaus director Walter Gropius designed his office as a showcase for the school. With its stark geometric shapes and patterns, it is severely modernist in style.

PAINTING WITH LIGHT

Art deco designers went wild with mirrors, glass and electric lighting, using them almost like paint or wallpaper to decorate walls and ceilings. Shimmering interiors were created for hotels, cinemas and office blocks and the new luxury ocean liners that were constructed in the post-war years. Usually the light bulbs themselves were hidden – often inside uplighters, sometimes behind vast glass panels.

This table lamp attracted huge interest from designers of the period. It was made in 1923–24 by two Bauhaus students, Wilhelm Wagenfeld (1900–90) and K.J. Tucker, and copies are still being produced today.

Hotel interiors were glittering display cases for the new look (Strand Palace Hotel, London, '30).

14

LIGHT SCULPTURES

Not all designers wanted to hide technology away – modernists deliberately incorporated it into their designs. They saw light bulbs not simply as things for producing light, but as objects with their own artistic appeal. The Dutch architect and furniture designer Gerrit Rietveld (1888–1964) led the way by creating sculptural fittings using tube-shaped light bulbs in the early '20s. The striking lamp that hung in Bauhaus director Walter Gropius' office was based on a design that Rietveld created for a doctor's clinic.

Nations competed to create the world's fastest and most luxurious ocean liners, and ship interiors displayed the very latest design ideas.

LEADING LIGHT

Created in 1932, the Anglepoise lamp is still in production today. The original was made from lacquered steel and Bakelite and designed deliberately for mass-production by Britain's Herbert Terry & Sons. The designer was a car engineer, George Carwardine (1887–1948), who based its movement on that of the human arm.

This poster promoted Terry's revolutionary new lamp.

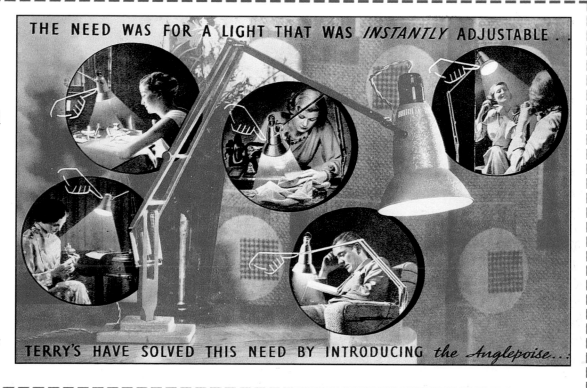

THE NEED WAS FOR A LIGHT THAT WAS *INSTANTLY* ADJUSTABLE .

TERRY'S HAVE SOLVED THIS NEED BY INTRODUCING *the Anglepoise...*

FURNITURE

The exciting development of the post-war years was the focus on designing objects specifically for mass-production. Until this time, most furniture had been expensively hand-crafted. In the 1920s designers began to exploit materials such as plywood which could be turned into sleek, modernist furniture on factory production lines.

Of course, not all new furniture was mass-produced. Wood was also handcrafted into modern designs.

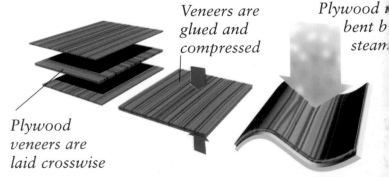

Geometric fabrics, a metal-and-glass chess table, and the abstract form of the arm-chair add up to a stylish art deco room.

WOOD-WORKING SKILLS

The technology for bending wood had been developed in the 18th century, but it was the Finn Alvar Aalto (1898–1976) who saw its potential for modernist design. He and his wife Aino Marsio experimented with bent wood and plywood during the '20s and Aalto's first piece, the Paimio chair, had been perfected by the early '30s.

FORGING A BONDING RELATIONSHIP

The technology for bending laminated wood was patented in 1841 by the German furniture-maker Michael Thonet (1796–1871). Thin sheets of wood (veneers) are glued together, pressure is used to laminate (bond) them, then steam is used to bend them. Plywood is stronger and was a later development. To make plywood, the veneers are placed so that the grain of each new sheet runs in the opposite direction to the grain on the sheet underneath.

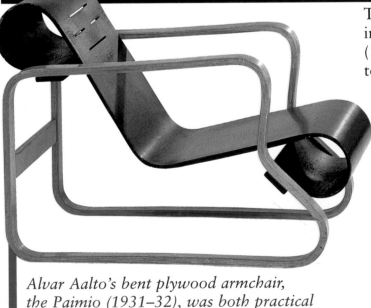

Alvar Aalto's bent plywood armchair, the Paimio (1931–32), was both practical to produce – and fairly comfortable to sit in!

Veneers are glued and compressed

Plywood bent b steam

Plywood veneers are laid crosswise

The simple design and construction of Marcel Breuer's tubular-steel Model B3 chair ('25) were ideal for airy, open-plan modernist rooms.

MACHINE AGE MATERIALS

Other designers found inspiration in metals such as steel and aluminium which until this time had mainly been used in the construction industry. The pioneer in this field was the Hungarian-born designer Marcel Breuer (1902–81). Breuer moved to Germany to train at the Bauhaus School, where at first he spent most of his time working with wood. His breakthrough came in '25, when he was so impressed by the strength and lightness of the tubular-steel frame of his new Adler bicycle that he made up his mind to apply the same techniques to furniture-making. Breuer's Model B3 (later named the Wassily) revolutionized the design of the armchair. Made from tubular steel and leather, it was simple, lightweight and strong – and completely unlike the heavy, bulky, upholstered armchairs of the past.

Many modernist designs are still in production today, including this out-door chair created in '38 by Swiss designer Hans Coray (b. 1906). Called the Landi, it is made from an aluminium alloy.

The cube-shaped, leather armchairs, the metal-and-leather footstool, and the strong, vertical and horizontal lines of the designs in this '30s sitting room are typically modernist.

DECORATIVE HOMES

In its early years, art deco stood for quality and luxury, for hand-crafted goods and expensive materials. Furniture was made from lacquered wood, for example, and decorated with inlays of exotic rosewood, ebony or mother-of-pearl, bronze or chrome mounts, and snake- or sharkskin coverings. Gradually, though, as art deco designs became more and more popular, low-price versions became available.

The bright, stylized designs of British ceramicist Clarice Cliff (1899–1972) were pure art deco – but at an affordable price.

AT HOME WITH HEAD-TO-TOE ART DECO

During the '30s art deco shapes and patterns trickled into every corner of people's homes, affecting everything from curtains to powder compacts. And the river became a torrent when mass-produced designs came on to the market, made from the cheap new plastics, Bakelite and Perspex.

THE MAGIC OF THE MOVIES

The 1920s and '30s were growth years for the film industry – by the time the first successful talkie, *The Jazz Singer*, was released in '27, well over 50 million people were going to films regularly each year. Film costume and set design helped to spread art deco styles to the bulk of the population.

The art deco sets for the 1929 film The Kiss *were inspired by Aztec and Mayan designs.*

An art deco coffee table is swamped with glass art deco ornaments!

PLASTIC FANTASTIC

Bakelite was the first industrially important plastic, and it was invented by the Belgian-born chemist Leo Baekelande in 1907. At first it was used as an alternative to rubber for insulation in plugs and switches, but by the '20s, manufacturers and designers were recognizing its wider potential. It had the shiny look that modern designers loved, and it came in a range of see-through or opaque colours – including butterscotch yellow, scarlet red, orange, violet blue and lime green, as well as brown and black. Soon everything from clocks, radios and jukeboxes to buttons, hairbrushes and jewellery was being made from Bakelite.

FAKE GLASS

Perspex was developed in '28 and started to appear on the market in the '30s. The great thing about this new plastic was that although it looked just like glass, it was tougher and far harder to break. Perspex is less heavy than glass, too, and in later years it was used for car and plane windscreens.

From candlesticks to salt-and-pepper pots, all of these '30s table ornaments are made from Perspex – it can be opaque as well as transparent.

PUTTING PLASTIC INTO PRODUCTION

Bakelite's great advantage was that it could be cast and moulded by machinery, and therefore mass-produced. It is made from two chemicals, phenol and formaldehyde, which solidify into a hard resin when heated. Any colour can be added to the mixture before moulding, and mixing two colours can produce a marbled effect.

Liquid phenol-formaldehyde is poured into a steel mould

The mould is baked in an oven

The hard Bakelite object is removed from the mould

Before the Bakelite Ekco AD65 hit the market in '34, radios came in square, wooden boxes. This revolutionary design was the work of British architect Wells Coates (1895–1958).

KITCHENWARE

Although there was massive unemployment during the 1920s and '30s, for the people who did have jobs, things had rarely been so good. And as standards of living rose, so did the demand for consumer goods.

FEEDING THE DEMAND

As more and more homes were connected to electricity, all sorts of electrical appliances were invented to make the most of the new power source – from electric kettles and irons, to hoovers, hairdryers and electric razors. Manufacturers soon recognized that the novelty of something just being electric would wear off, though, and that one way of expanding the market for their products would be to change and update designs regularly. The gadget itself would not be new, but it would be desirable because it looked new.

Women might have won new freedom during the war, but the majority were still full-time housewives and mothers.

A page from a department store catalogue of 1939 shows the wide range of electrical goods on sale.

DESIGNING FOR INDUSTRY

Probably the first artist to apply his skills to industrial design was the German architect and designer Peter Behrens (1868–1940), who began advising the German electrical company AEG in 1907. By the early '30s, however, the American economy was recovering from the Wall Street Crash of '29, and the United States was leading the world in the design and production of industrial goods.

British pottery manufacturers T.G. Green introduced their cheap, functional Cornish Kitchenware range in '27 because their factory workers' jobs were threatened by the depression.

Made from shiny Bakelite plastic and metal, the Moka Express is an art deco classic. It was designed in 1930, but was not mass-produced until after World War II.

MODERN KITCHENS

If the modernist home was a machine for living, then the kitchen was a laboratory for the scientific storage and preparation of food. Above all else, kitchens had to be streamlined and hygienic. By the '30s, sleek, built-in units were beginning to replace the old free-standing cupboards, while metal cookers and refrigerators were coated in enamel for easy cleaning. No single item of kitchenware was left untouched by industrial designers. Everything was restyled to give it the new look – toasters, food mixers, crockery, cutlery, saucepans, even kitchen trays, clocks and radios.

The shiny surfaces so loved by post-war designers were achieved by coating metal either in enamel, or in another metal such as chrome. Enamel is powdered glass which is heated until it melts on to the metal. Electrolysis is used to coat metals in chrome (the process is called electroplating). When an electric current is passed through a solution containing chrome, the positive chrome ions are attracted to the cathode and a thin layer is deposited on the object being plated.

An electric current travels from cathode to anode

Anode (+)

Cathode (-) attached to the object to be plated

Positive chrome ions are attracted to the cathode

Solution containing ions of chrome

21

When the Aga oven was invented in 1922, its clean lines were the cutting edge of modernism. It was designed by the Swedish engineer Gustaf Dalén (1869–1937).

Raymond Loewy (1893–1986) was one of the United States' leading industrial designers – he restyled everything from cars to Coca-Cola bottles. His Coldspot Super Six refrigerator ('35) was one of the first consumer products to be given a sleek, streamlined shape.

ROAD MACHINES

Mass-production techniques had developed during the 19th century, but it was not until American car manufacturer Henry Ford introduced the assembly line in 1913 that manufacturing became truly efficient. Ford's assembly line allowed him to drop the price of his Model T car from US$950 in 1908 to less than US$300 by the mid-20s.

Raymond Loewy restyled the US Greyhound Corporation's bus fleet in '40. The banded bodywork adds to the sense of streamlined speed.

22

MARKET LEADERS

Around 15 million Model T Fords had been sold by the mid-'20s, and the Ford Motor Company had completely cornered the market for the family car. However, this stranglehold was about to be broken – by a new technique known as 'styling'. In '27, General Motors made engineer Harley Earl (1893–1969) head of their new Art and Color Section (from '37, the Styling Section), and for the next 32 years Earl was responsible for the design of all the company's cars. Earl believed that unlike Model T Fords (which were always black and still looked exactly the same as they had done in 1908), a car should be visually appealing, or stylish. He also backed the idea of introducing a new design as soon as an old model's appeal wore off.

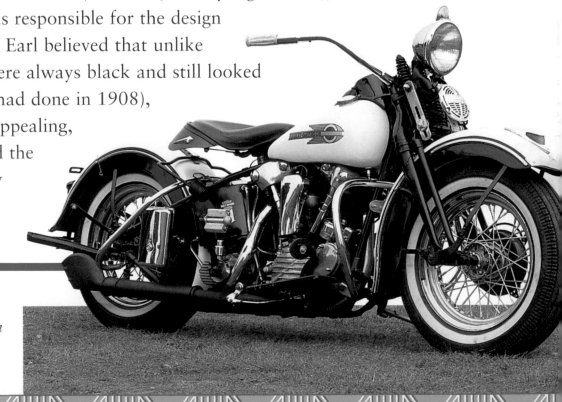

Lean machine – the stretched body and sleek chromework of this 1939 Harley-Davidson motorbike screams speed (first model built in 1903).

Designed by Carl Breer and launched in '34, the Chrysler Airflow was one of the first streamlined cars.

THE SHAPE OF SPEED

A stylish car had to look modern, and speed was one of the key symbols of post-war modernity. Engineers had found that machines move faster if they have a smooth, streamlined shape, and industrial designers streamlined everything in sight – even static objects like pencil sharpeners. When it came to road machines, streamlining meant curved bodies, bumpers and radiators, slanted windscreens, and sleek, shiny chromework.

23

GOING WITH THE FLOW

When a machine moves, it is slowed by the resistance of the air or water it travels through. This resistance is called drag, and reducing it makes machines move faster and use less fuel. Streamlining is shaping an object to reduce drag. Smooth curves help, but the ideal streamlined shape is a teardrop. A few industrial designers – including the Americans Buckminster Fuller and Norman Bel Geddes (1893–1958) – designed teardrop-shaped vehicles, but most designs were thought so futuristic that they were never put into mass-production.

Buckminster Fuller's three-wheeled Dymaxion car ('33–34) is a fine example of the streamlined, teardrop shape.

Norman Bel Geddes photographed in '39 with a model of one of his futuristic designs, a teardrop-shaped bus.

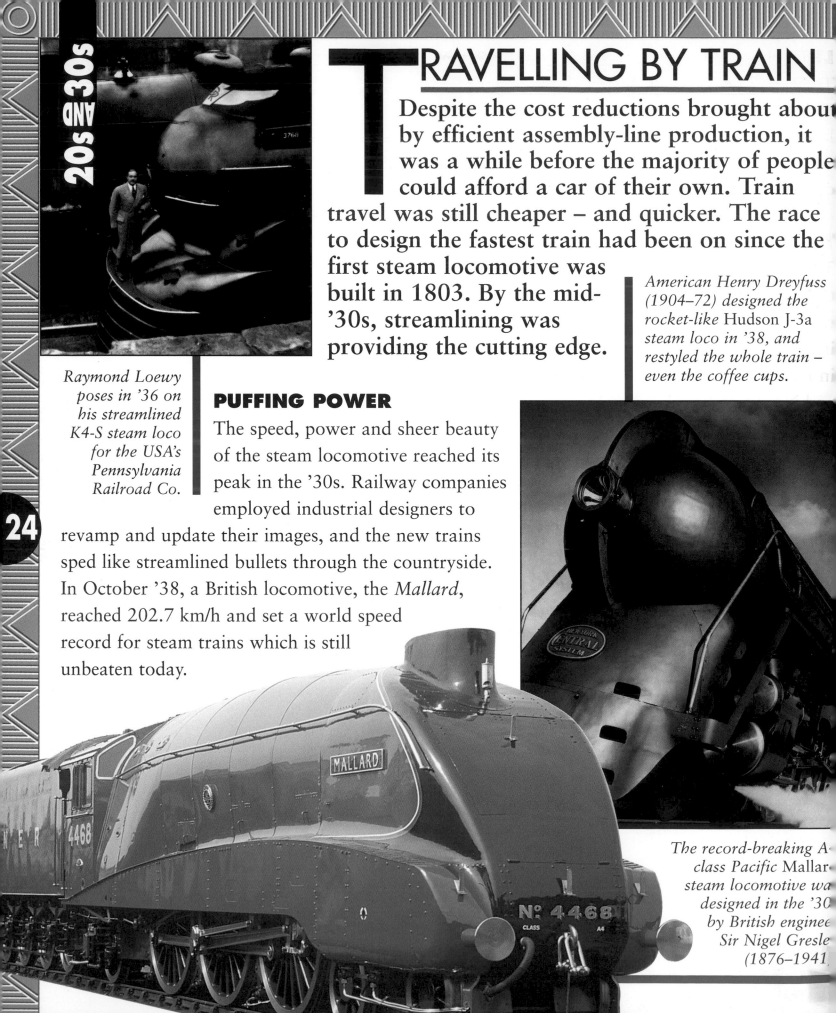

TRAVELLING BY TRAIN

Despite the cost reductions brought about by efficient assembly-line production, it was a while before the majority of people could afford a car of their own. Train travel was still cheaper – and quicker. The race to design the fastest train had been on since the first steam locomotive was built in 1803. By the mid-'30s, streamlining was providing the cutting edge.

Raymond Loewy poses in '36 on his streamlined K4-S steam loco for the USA's Pennsylvania Railroad Co.

American Henry Dreyfuss (1904–72) designed the rocket-like Hudson J-3a steam loco in '38, and restyled the whole train – even the coffee cups.

PUFFING POWER

The speed, power and sheer beauty of the steam locomotive reached its peak in the '30s. Railway companies employed industrial designers to revamp and update their images, and the new trains sped like streamlined bullets through the countryside. In October '38, a British locomotive, the *Mallard*, reached 202.7 km/h and set a world speed record for steam trains which is still unbeaten today.

24

The record-breaking A-class Pacific Mallard *steam locomotive was designed in the '30s by British engineer Sir Nigel Gresley (1876–1941).*

LETTING THE TRAIN TAKE THE STRAIN

Train interiors were also restyled, particularly in the United States. When American travellers grew tired of lazing about in a plush armchair in an air-conditioned compartment, they could visit an open-view observation car or have a drink in a chrome-plated cocktail lounge.

THE END OF AN ERA

The days of the coal-fired steam train were numbered, though, as nations switched to cleaner, electric-powered rail systems. The first electric train had been demonstrated in 1879, and by the 1930s electric trains were widespread in Europe – particularly in countries such as Switzerland and Norway where hydroelectric power stations pumped out cheap, renewable, pollution-free energy.

THE RISE OF THE DIESEL-ELECTRIC TRAIN

The first diesel-electric trains began running in the '30s. They were cleaner and more fuel efficient than steam trains, converting over 25 per cent of their fuel into hauling power. Steam trains converted less than 10 per cent of their fuel, coal. In a diesel-electric train, the diesel engine drives an electricity generator, which powers traction motors that drive the wheels. The traction motors are usually in bogies (the sub-frame that carries a set of wheels), spaced along the entire length of the train.

Germany's two-car Flying Hamburger *was one of the first diesel-electric trains. On its maiden run in Köln in '32, its average speed was 125 km/h.*

25

The first American diesel-electric train, the streamlined Pioneer Zephyr *('34), was also the first with shiny, stainless-steel bodywork. Its top speed was 177 km/h.*

AIR TRAVEL

The 1920s and '30s were record-breaking decades for aviators. Charles Lindbergh made history by completing the first solo flight across the Atlantic in '27. Just one year later, Charles Smith and C.T. Ulm achieved the first trans-Pacific flight, and in '32 Amelia Earhart became the first woman to carry out a solo Atlantic crossing.

By the mid-'30s, customers of the British national airline company Imperial Airways were still flying in slow, unstreamlined biplanes.

ONWARDS AND UPWARDS

Sports flying was also popular, and aviators competed to win cash prizes and trophies for flying higher and fastest than ever before. Many of the most important speed records were set by competitors in the international Schneider Trophy races for seaplanes – winners took the world air speed record from 452 km/h in '23 to 689 km/h in '31. At the same time, the race to be the fastest in the air prompted technological breakthroughs, as engineers worked to create lighter and more streamlined planes.

In '31 the Schneider Trophy was won outright by the British team in this Supermarine S-6B seaplane. The streamlined design of the S-6B influenced that of the World War II Spitfire.

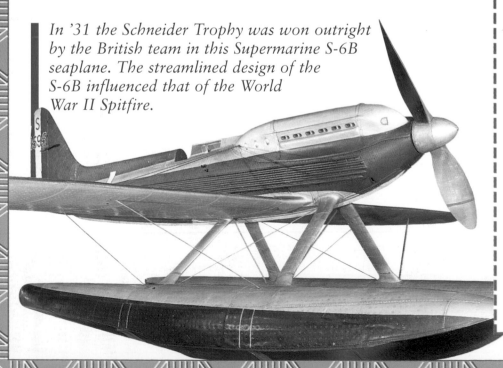

PIGGYBACK LIFT-OFF

The greatest obstacle to trans-Atlantic passenger flights was designing an airliner that could carry enough fuel. British engineer Major Robert Mayo came up with one solution – reducing the amount of fuel used by take-off. A large, powerful flying boat helped launch a smaller plane into the air. Once airborne, the smaller plane could make a long journey on relatively little fuel.

Mayo's plane made its one and only record-breaking Atlantic crossing in '39.

With its upholstered seats, luggage racks and curtains, the cabin of this 1934 airliner was the height of comfort and luxury. The first airline passengers had sat on ordinary wicker chairs, and fought off the cold with overcoats and hot water bottles.

SPREADING THE LOAD

Early planes were mainly made from wood and canvas. They were light, but neither streamlined nor strong. Experiments with streamlined metal designs began during World War I, and by the early '20s they had resulted in a revolutionary new way of making 'stressed-skin' aircraft from duralumin (a lightweight aluminium alloy developed in 1908–12).

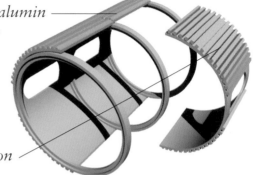

A skin of thin duralumin sheets is riveted to the plane skeleton

The stressed-skin bears much of the load that before had been carried only by the skeleton

GAINING THE FREEDOM OF THE SKIES

The air had belonged largely to pilots until 1919 – only a lucky few passengers had ever travelled on board planes. When regular passenger flights did start up after the war, the only planes were noisy, converted bombers. There was not enough money to invest in purpose-built airliners until after the first large national airline companies were founded in the mid-'20s. Many of these early airliners were flying boats, because of the scarcity of landing strips outside Europe and the United States. And it was some time before technological breakthroughs such as the stressed-skin structure were adopted, and the shape of airliners evolved from the boxy bi-winged plane into the streamlined monoplane.

Designed for the American Douglas Company by engineer Arthur E. Raymond in '35, the Douglas DC-3 had the most modern stressed-skin, streamlined structure. It was to become the world's most successful airliner.

27

POSTERS & PACKAGING

With efficient mass-production came the need for mass-marketing, and the post-war years saw an increasing awareness of the importance of advertizing. In the United States, for example, the '20s saw a number of professional advertizing agencies being set up in and around New York's Madison Avenue.

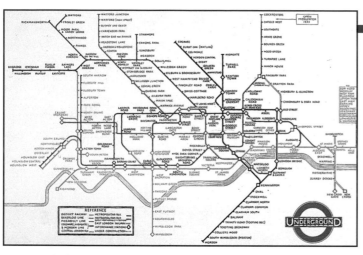

The abstract, geometric design of the 1933 London Underground map was based on electrical circuit diagrams by its creator, British engineering draughtsman Henry C. Beck (1901–74).

Frenchman Paul Colin (1892–1985) designed this poster for the 1925 show that introduced Europe to the authentic music of black America.

AT THE STROKE OF A PEN

The design of posters and packaging had to be as up-to-date as the goods and services they advertized. Sans-serif typefaces looked clean, modern and streamlined, and the '20s saw a creative explosion of them, particularly from Bauhaus designers such as Herbert Bayer (1900–85).

British railway companies commissioned contemporary artists to create a series of striking advertizements.

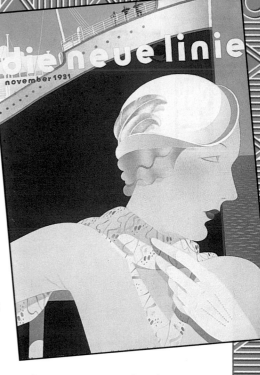

The message of this 1931 German shipping line poster is that taking an ocean voyage is as fashionable as cropped hair and a cloche hat!

THE PLEASURES OF TRAVEL

Very few people thought of travelling any great distance for a holiday at this time, so it was in the interests of transport companies to advertize their services. Many of the most striking posters of the period were created by the French graphic artist A.M. Cassandre (1901–68). The clean sans-serif typography, simple strong colours and stylized artwork of Cassandre's posters had a huge influence on graphic designers throughout the world.

GETTING A MESSAGE ACROSS

Another growing trend was the use of a slogan or a visual logo to build loyalty to a particular brand. Companies employed industrial designers and advertizing agencies to streamline their packaging, and to devise catchy slogans and company logos. In France, Cassandre created a poster series for the Dubonnet company, for example, while in the United States, Raymond Loewy restyled the packaging for Lucky Strike cigarettes.

Cassandre's 1927 poster promoting the streamlined Etoile du Nord *train is one of the world's best-known advertizements.*

In Britain, a series of posters sold the idea that Guinness was good for you.

GLOSSARY

ART DECO A post-World-War-I decorative arts and architecture style, characterized by strong, bright colours and geometric shapes and patterns.

ART NOUVEAU A decorative arts and architecture style of the 1880s–1900s, characterized by stylized plant and animal motifs and sinuous, curling patterns.

BAKELITE The trade name of the first synthetic plastic.

CONSUMER GOODS Products bought to satisfy personal needs.

DEPRESSION A period when there is a severe slump in business and industrial activity, and a rise in unemployment.

FASCISM A political movement or system, which suppresses democracy and enforces state control of all aspects of society.

INDUSTRIAL DESIGNER Someone who designs products that will be made by machines.

LASTEX An elastic fibre first sold in 1931. Silk, wool or rayon was wound round a rubber core.

MASS-PRODUCTION The manufacture of standardized products in large quantities, usually by machines.

MODERNISM An international movement in architecture and design that emerged in the early 20th century. Rejecting historical styles and unnecessary decoration, modernists believed that the appearance of an object or building should be determined by its use.

PERSPEX The trade name of a tough, light, see-through plastic first marketed in the 1930s.

PREFABRICATE To manufacture parts of a building – such as windows, stairs and reinforced concrete sections – so that later on they can be assembled quickly at the construction site.

RAYON An artificial, silk-like material made from wood chips or pulp (named in 1924).

REINFORCED CONCRETE Concrete strengthened by having steel bars or wires embedded in it.

SERIF A short stroke at the tip of a printed letter. Sans-serif type doesn't have the stroke.

STREAMLINED With the sleek, curved shape that allows an object to move smoothly through air or water.

VENEER A thin layer of wood.

30

DESIGN HIGHLIGHTS

- *Chanel makes 'yachting pants' for women* 1
- *'Chanel No 5' perfume launched* 1
- *Aga oven designed by Dalén* 1
- 1
- *Rietveld's sculptural, exposed-lightbulb lamp* 1
- *Paris exhibition of decorative arts* 1
- *Breuer's B32 (Cesca) tubular steel chair* 1
- *Buckminster Fuller's Dymaxion House* 1
- 1
- *Schiaparelli's first full collection* 1
- *Van Alen's Chrysler Building completed* 1
- *Le Corbusier's Villa Savoye* 1
- *Carwardine's Anglepoise lamp* 1
- *Bauhaus design school closed by Nazis* 1
- *Wells Coates' Ekco AD65 radio* 1
- *Loewy's Coldspot fridge •Douglas DC3* 1
- *Volkswagen Beetle designed by Porsche* 1
- *Dreyfuss' streamlined Hudson J-3a train* 1
- *New York World's Fair held* 1

TIMELINE

	WORLD EVENTS	TECHNOLOGY	FAMOUS PEOPLE	ART & MEDIA
0	•USA: women get vote	•Electric hairdryer first made	•Joan of Arc canonized	•D.H. Lawrence: Women in Love
1	•Chinese communist party founded	•Insulin discovered	•Marie Stopes opens Britain's first birth control clinic	•Rudolph Valentino stars in The Sheik
2	•Russia becomes USSR	•Choc-ice (Eskimo pie) invented	•Tutankhamun's tomb opened	•James Joyce: Ulysses •T.S. Eliot: The Wasteland
3	•Italy: Mussolini seizes power	•Autogiro (early helicopter) flown in Spain		•Cecil B. de Mille: The Ten Commandments
4	•Britain: first Labour goverment elected	•First motorway opens, in Italy •Rayon named	•Death of Lenin	•Gershwin: Rhapsody in Blue
5		•Scotch tape invented	•George Bernard Shaw wins Nobel Prize for Literature	•F. Scott Fitzgerald: The Great Gatsby
6	•Britain: General Strike	•J.L. Baird: first television •Godard: first rocket	•Gertrude Ederle swims the Channel •Valentino dies	•Fritz Lang's futuristic Metropolis
7	•German stock market collapses	•First Volvo car made •Polyesters first used	•Charles Lindbergh is first to fly the Atlantic solo	•First successful 'talkie', The Jazz Singer
8	•USSR: Stalin's first five-year plan	•Discovery of penicillin •Perspex first made	•Death of Emeline Pankhurst	•Brecht: Threepenny Opera •First Micky Mouse cartoon
9	•USA: Wall Street Crash; Hoover elected president			•Mondrian: Composition in a Square
0	•India: Gandhi leads Salt March protest	•Planet Pluto identified •Turbojet engine patented	•Amy Johnson is first woman to fly to Australia	•Dietrich stars in The Blue Angel
1	•Japanese army occupies Chinese Manchuria	•Lastex yarn introduced		•Dali: Limp Watches •Cagney in The Public Enemy
2	•Nazis take control of Reichstag (parliament)	•Polythene created •First radio telescope	•Amelia Earhart flies solo across the Atlantic	•Huxley: Brave New World
3	•Hitler in power, as Chancellor of Germany	•Lemaître proposes Big Bang theory		•Fay Wray in King Kong •Garbo in Queen Christina
4	•China: Communists led by Mao on Long March	•Nylon invented •Cat's-eye road studs first used	•Shirley Temple wins an Oscar aged six	•Henry Miller: Tropic of Cancer
5	•Italy invades Abyssinia (Ethiopia)	•First TV broadcasting station built, in Germany	•Malcolm Campbell sets 300 mph land speed record	•Fred Astaire & Ginger Rogers star in Top Hat
6	•Spanish Civil War begins •Edward VIII abdicates		•Jessie Owens stars at the Berlin Olympics	•Ben Nicholson: White Relief
7	•India: Congress Party wins elections	•Ballpoint pen invented •Polyurethanes discovered		•Picasso: Guernica •Disney: Snow White
8	•Germany & Austria unite (Anschluss)	•Teflon discovered		•H. Moore: Recumbent Figure •First Superman comic strip
9	•Spanish Civil War ends •World War II begins	•Heinkel built first jet aircraft	•Sigmund Freud dies	•Steinbeck: The Grapes of Wrath

INDEX